# Still Life

Claude Serre

# Still Life

Methuen

A METHUEN PAPERBACK

First published in Great Britain in 1985
by Methuen London Ltd
11 New Fetter Lane, London EC4P 4EE
Copyright © Claude Serre and Editions Jacques Glénat 1981
Design by Georges Lacroix
Made and printed in Great Britain

ISBN 0 413 58830 0

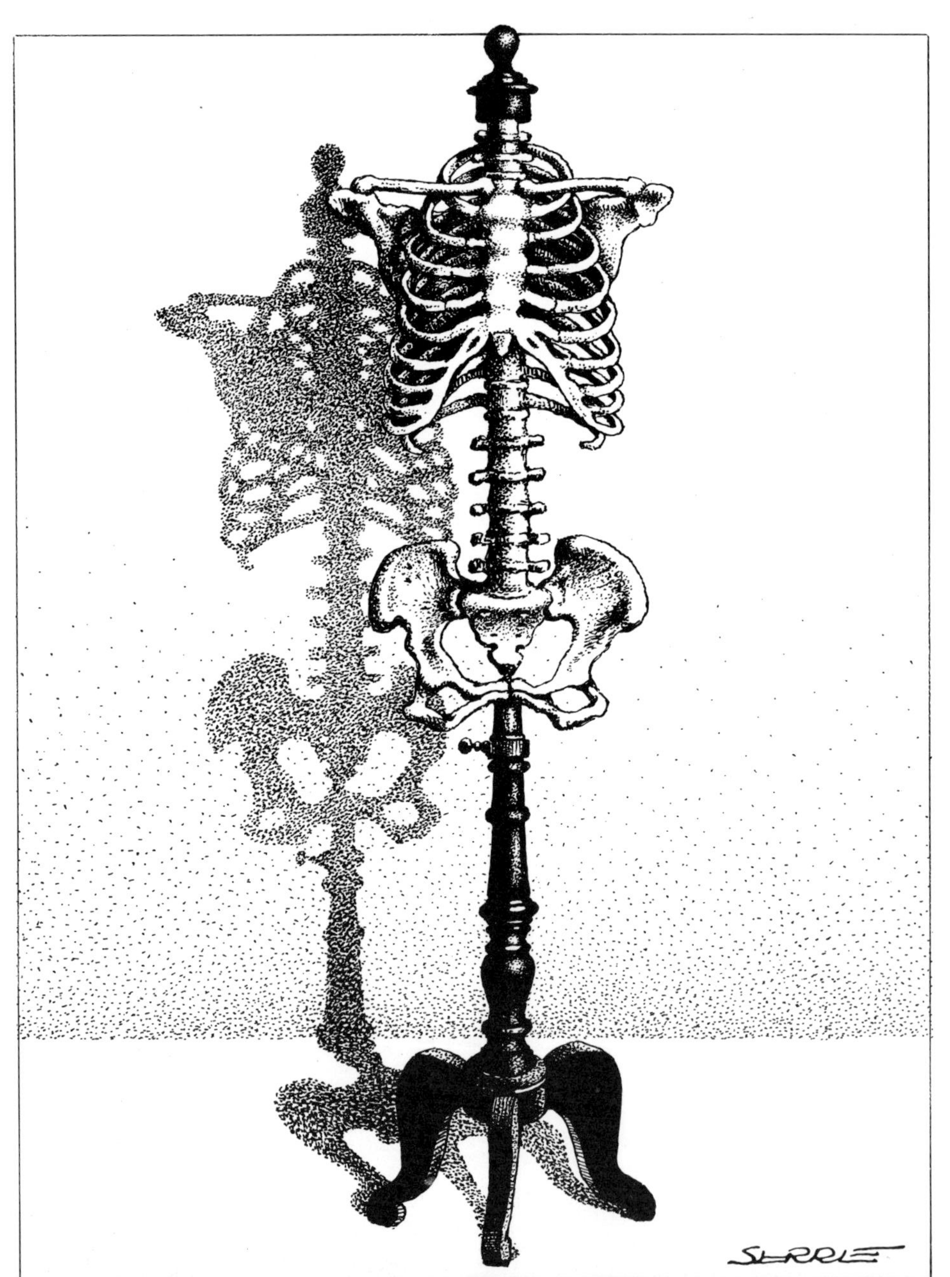

To be
or not to be,
that is
the question.

SERRE

We're giving the place a facelift
to attract the younger customer

GOOD
MORNING

GOT A LIGHT?
RUM

SERRE

EMERGENCY EXIT
SERRE

Could you pick up
a loaf for us?

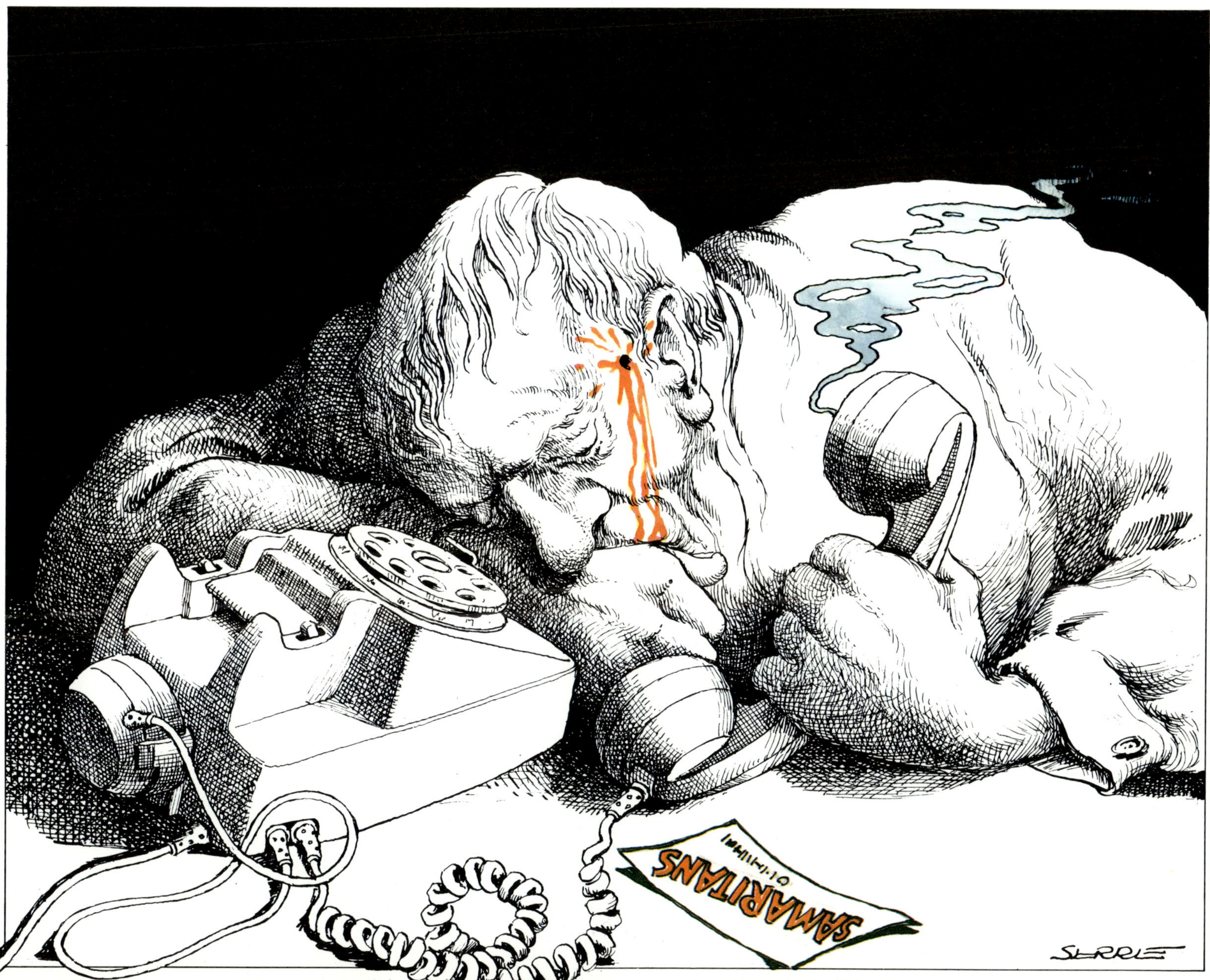
SAMARITANS
SERRE

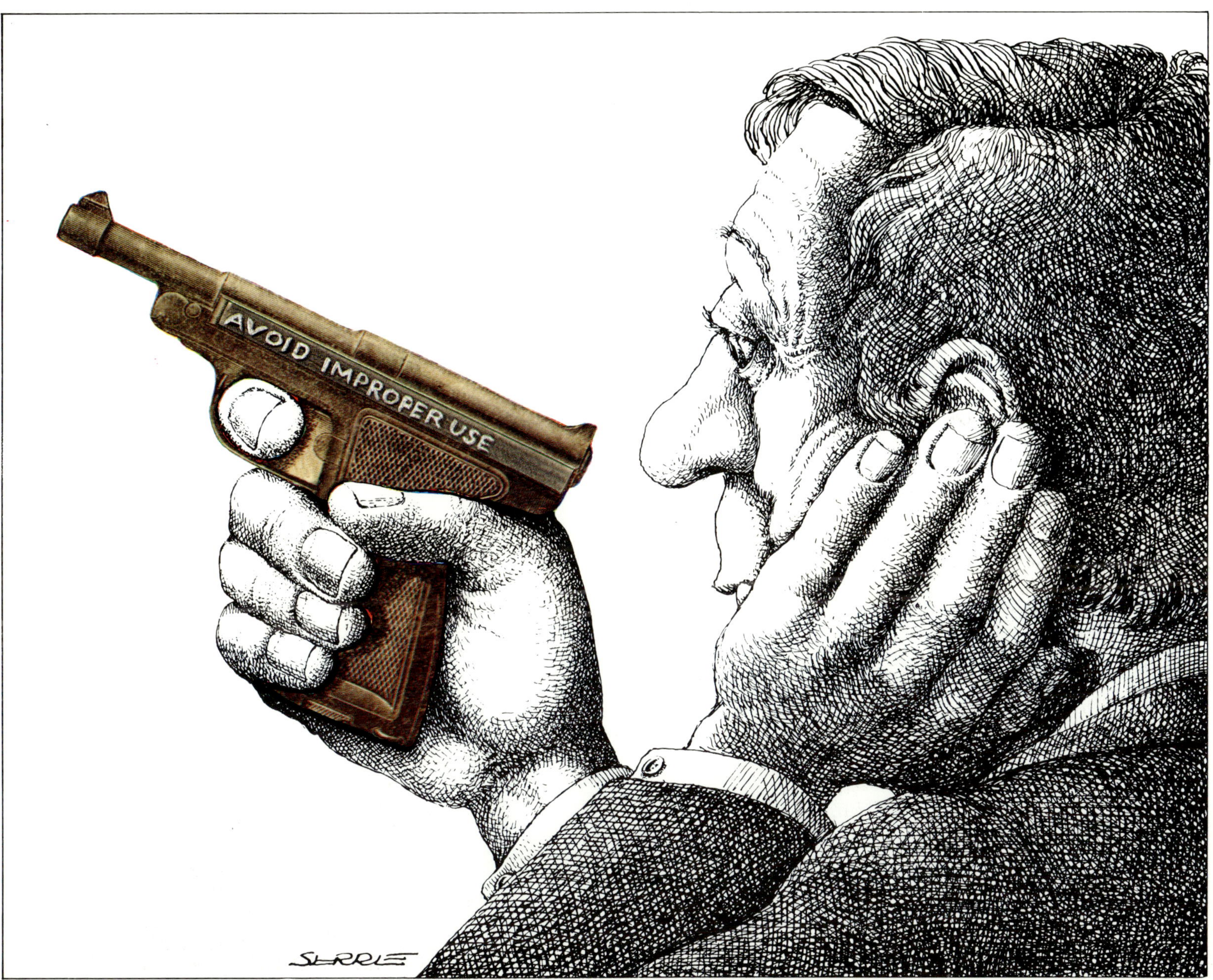

AVOID IMPROPER USE
SERRE

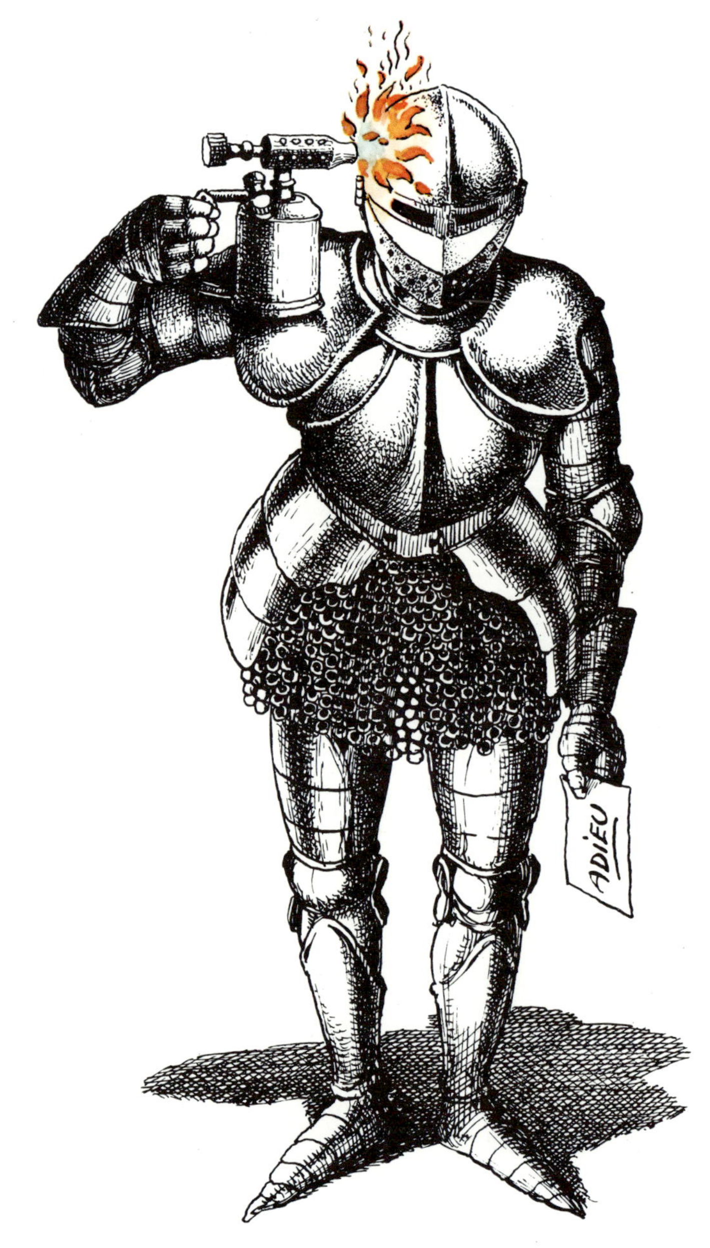

ADIEU

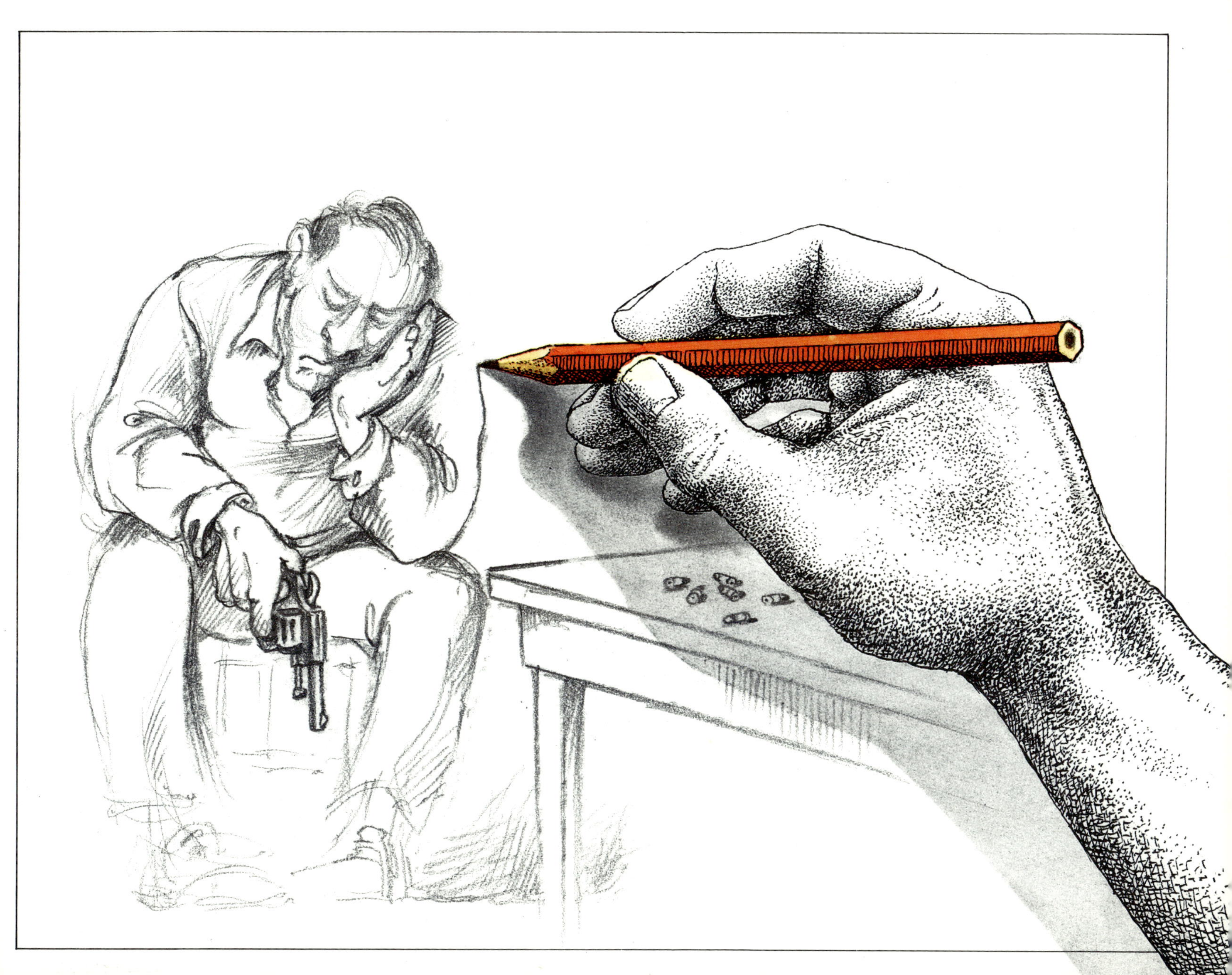

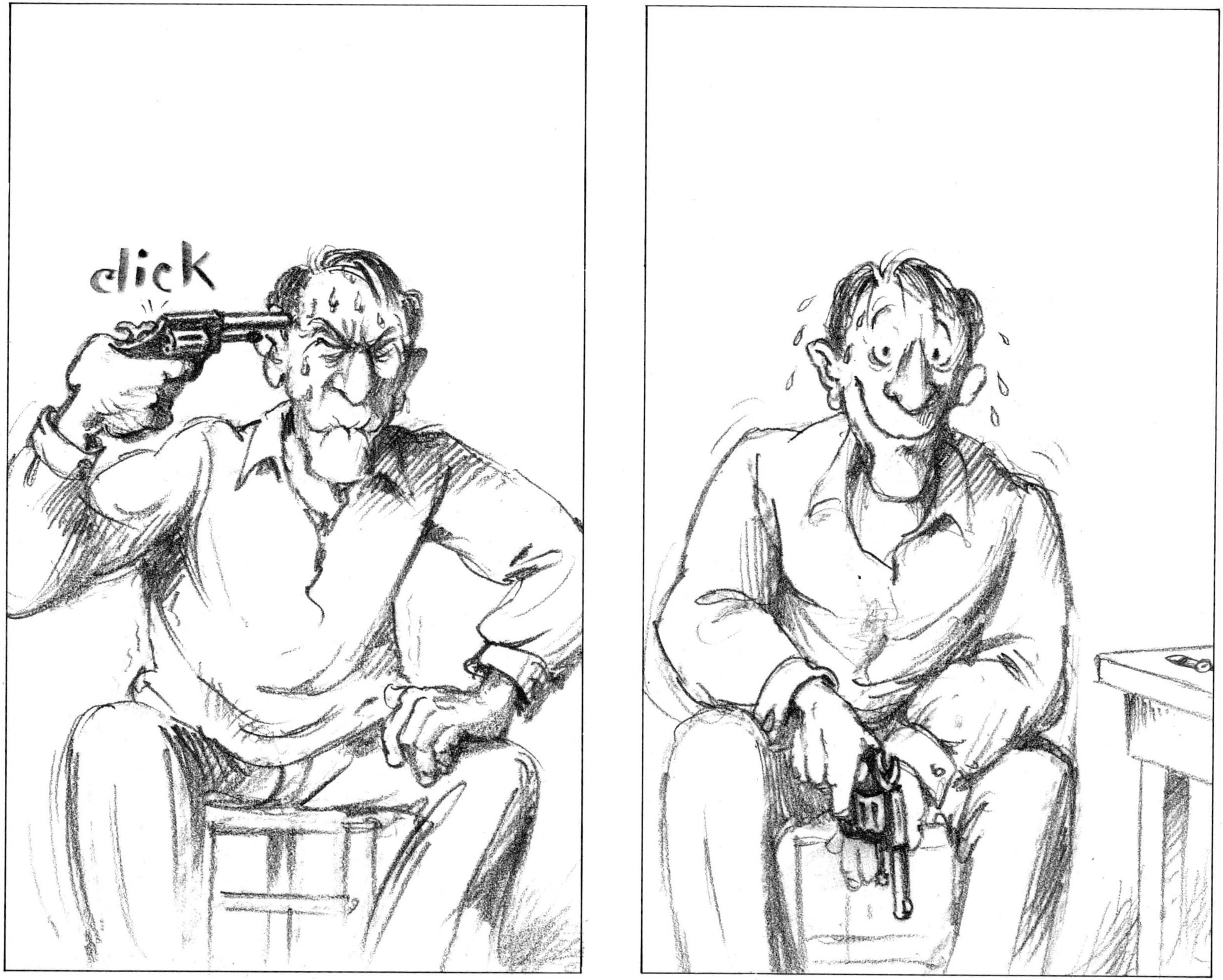

click

Oh no! That's the door opposite
B. SMITH
BRIAN SMITH

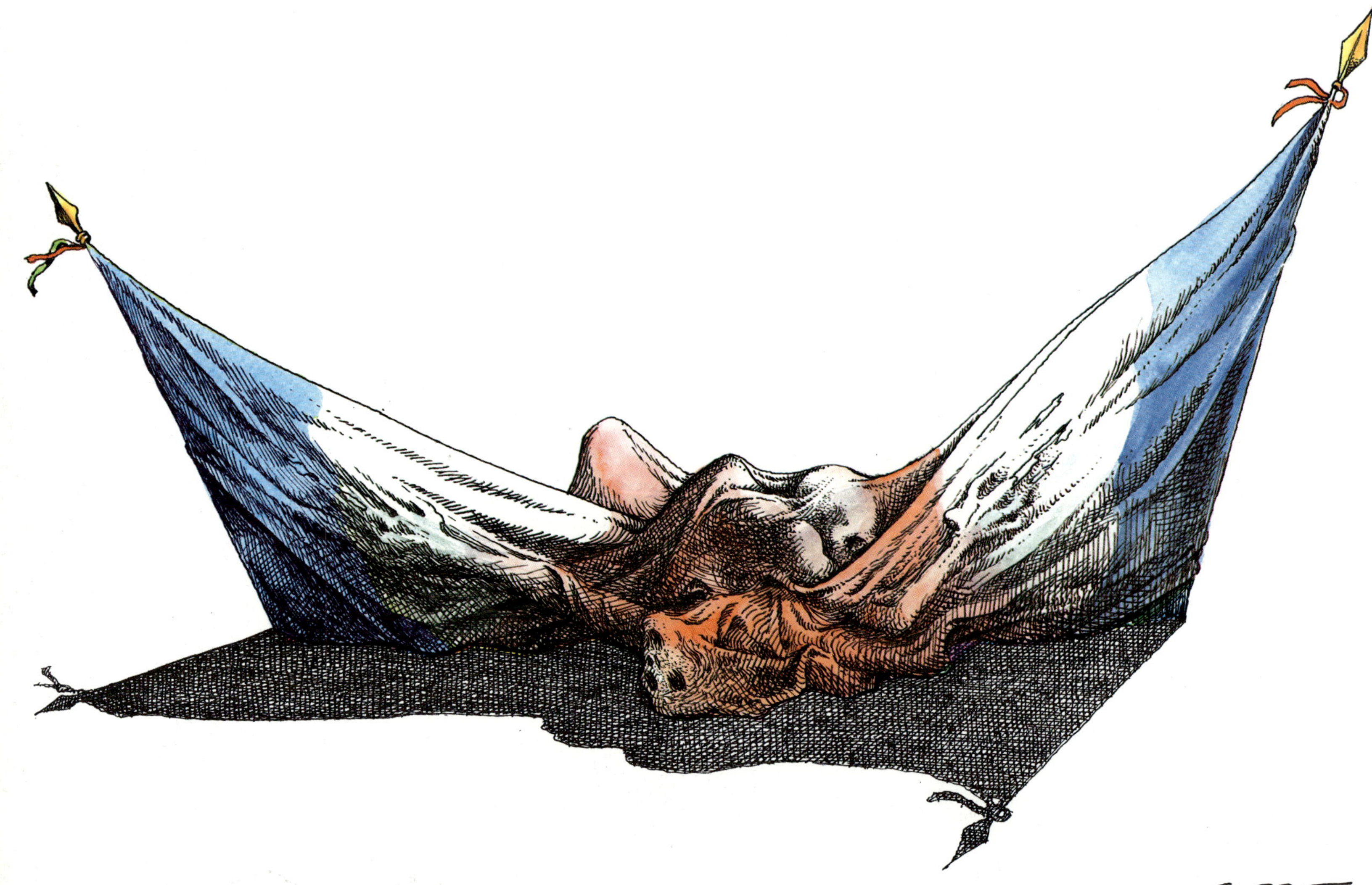

TO
THE BATTLEFIELD

SERRE

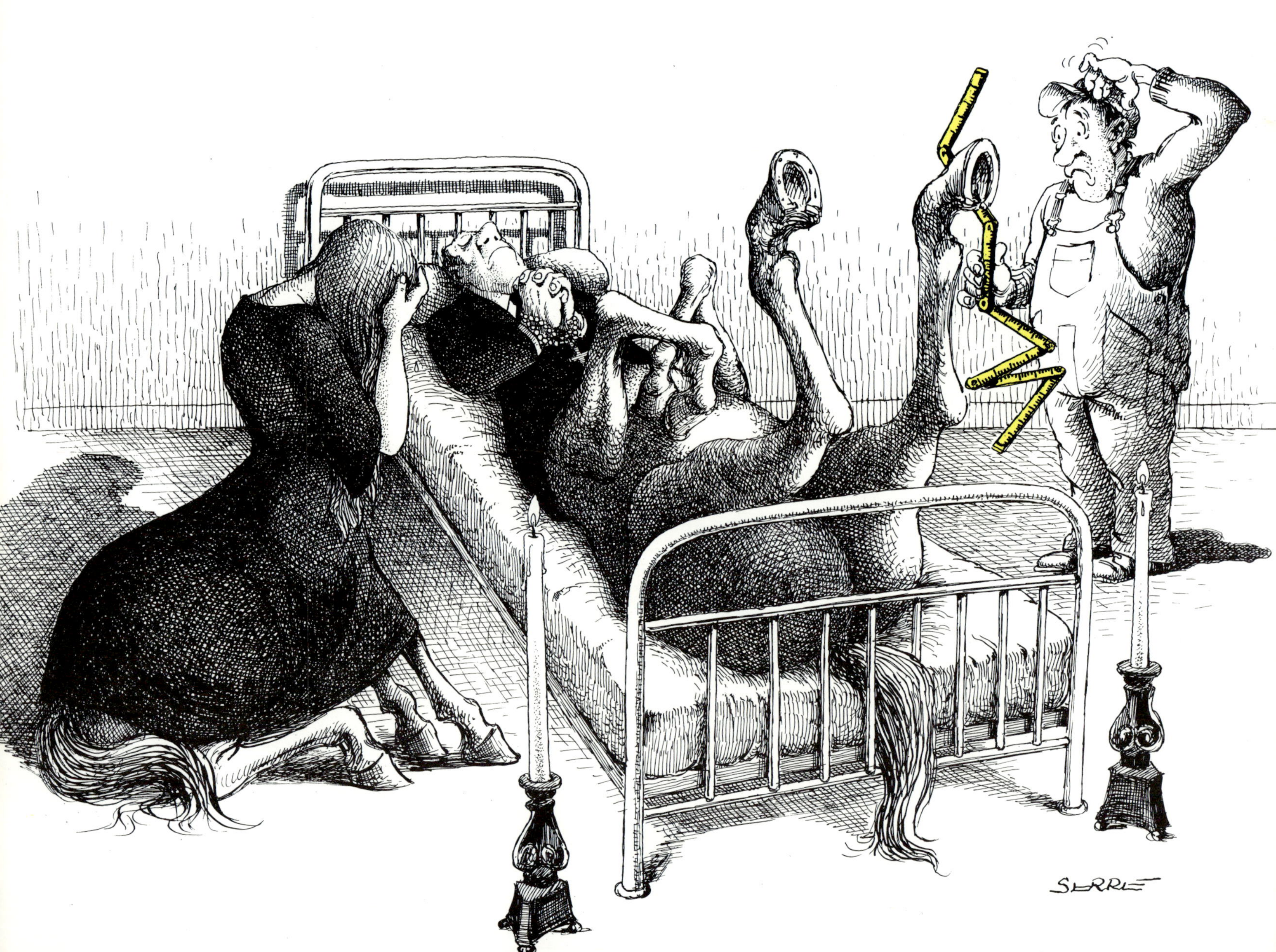

HOTEL
UNDERTAKERS
SERRE

SERRE

SERRE

Ping
25
ST PETER
SERRLE

TERNAL SORROW

FAMILLE
RECARD
ERNEST
LAPOTRE
1920-1971
SERRE

P. CATCHPOLE
SOLICITOR

LAST WILL & TESTAMENT

I, John Robinson
LAST WILL & TESTAMENT

LAST WILL & TESTAMENT
I, John
Robin

JONES FAMILY
FOR SALE:
LONG LEASE
SERRE

SERRE
EMILE DUGENOU
1896-1980
HERE LIES
GUSTAVE
1879

SERRE

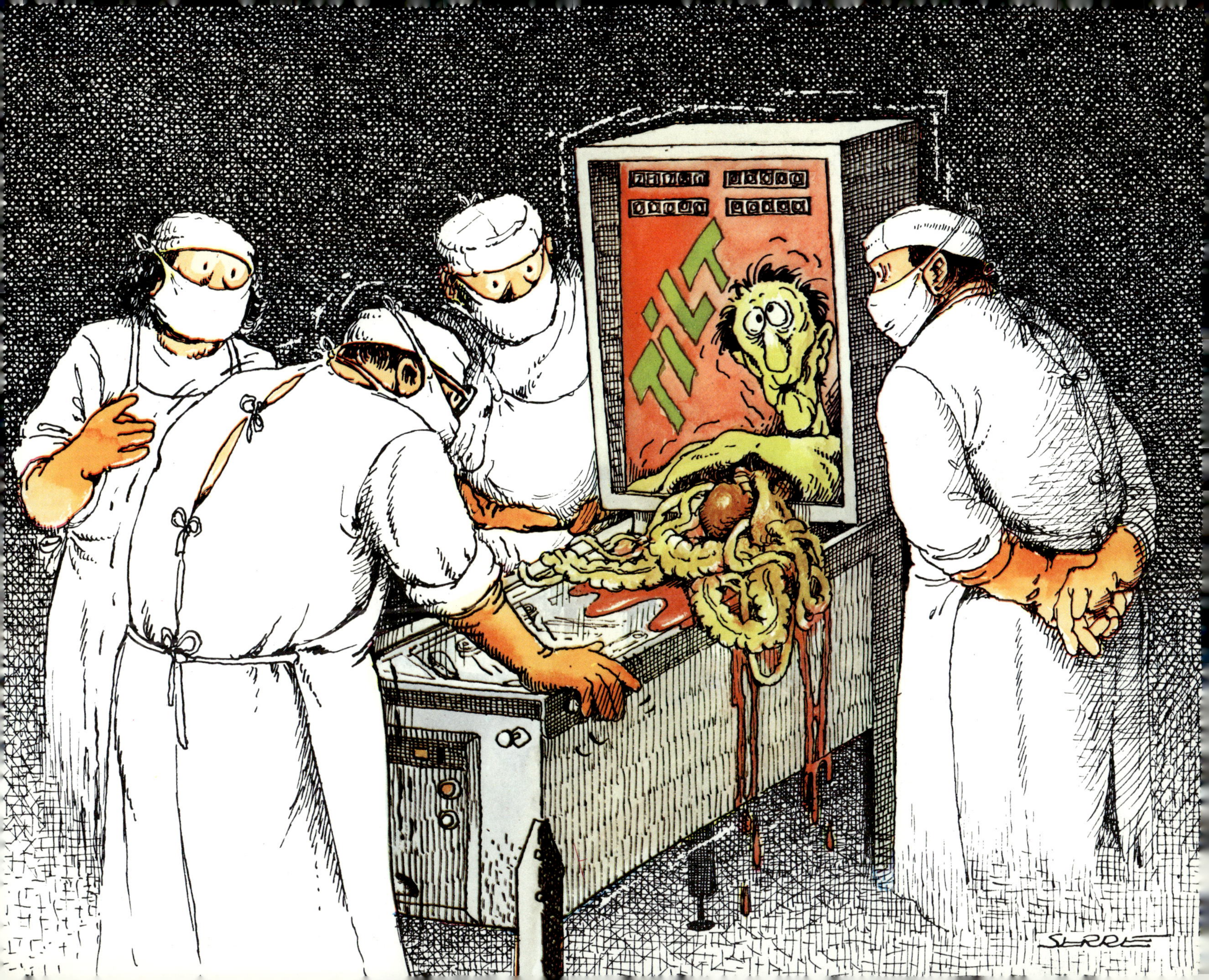

TILT

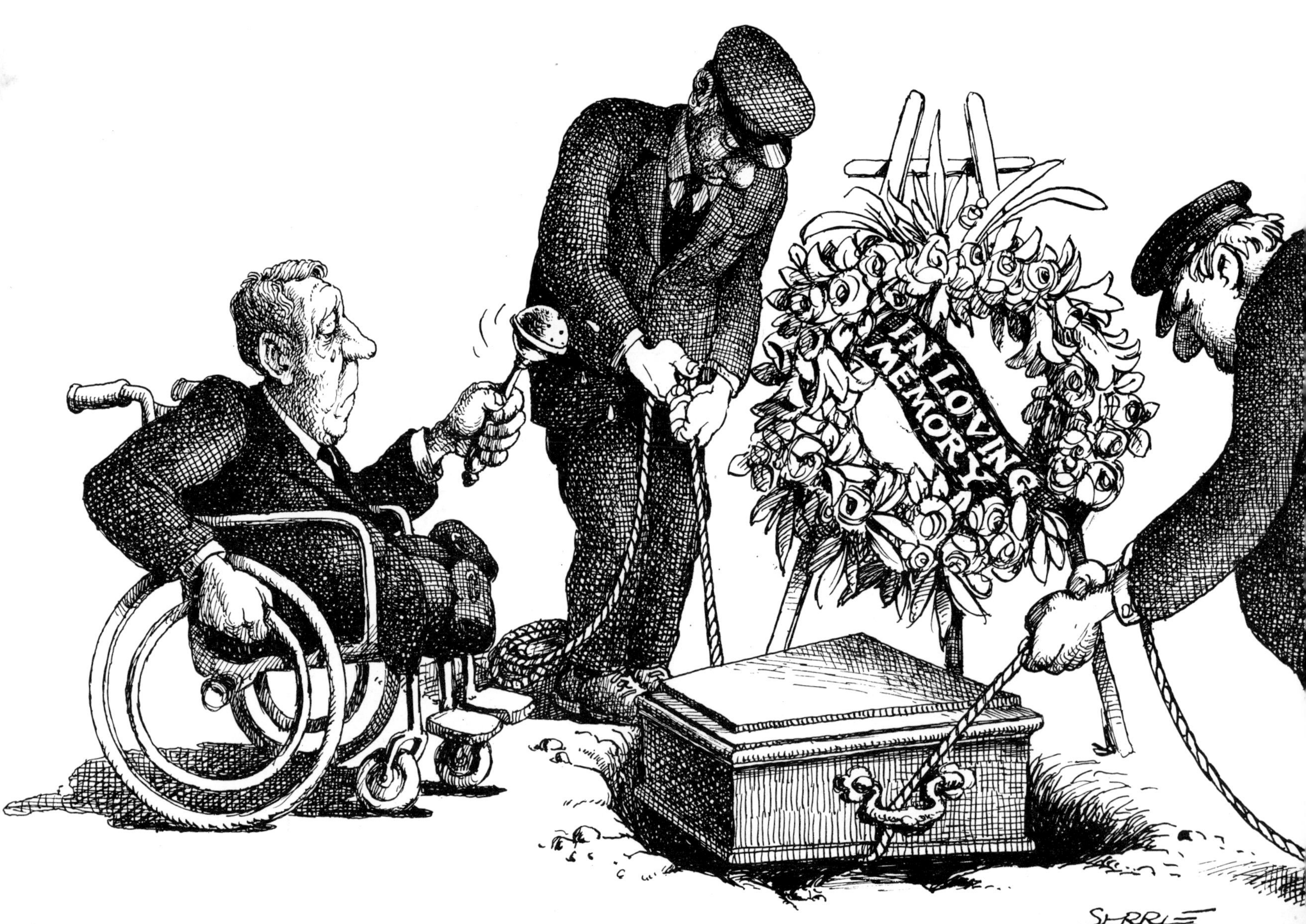

IN LOVING MEMORY
SERRLE

MY BELOVED WIFE
SERRE

DON'T DISTVRB

THE
END